|| Dedicated to All Wisdom Seekers Around the World ||

BEYOND THE FLAMES

THE UNSEEN REALMS OF MANIKARNIKA GHAT AND THE SECRET TEACHINGS OF THE AGHORI

DR. JAGADEESH PILLAI

Made with ♥ on the Notion Press Platform
www.notionpress.com

Contents

Contents

Prayer

"Om tryambakam yajamahe sugandhim pushtivardhanam Urvarukamiva bandhanan mrityor mokshiya maamritat"

We worship the three-eyed Lord who is fragrant and nourishing. May He release us from the bonds of death, just as the ripe cucumber is released from the vine.

About The Author Of The Book

Dr. Jagadeesh Pillai is a renowned Guinness World Record holder, writer, and researcher hailing from Varanasi, also known as the abode of Lord Shiva. With a Ph.D. in Vedic Science and a range of creative ideas and achievements, he is a true polymath. Although his roots can be traced back to Kerala, the people of Varanasi hold him in high regard and affectionately consider him one of their own.

Dr. Pillai has achieved four Guinness World Records in the following subjects:

1. "Script to Screen" - In this record, Dr. Pillai produced and directed an animation film within the shortest time possible, breaking the previous record set by Canadians. He has also received numerous national and international awards and recognitions for this achievement.

2. Longest Line of Postcards - For this record, Dr. Pillai created a line of 16,300 postcards on the occasion of the 163rd anniversary of Indian Postal Day. The event also included a questionnaire about the Indian flag.

3. Largest Poster Awareness Campaign - Dr. Pillai designed an awareness campaign on the subject of "Beti Bachao - Beti Padhao" (Save the Girl Child - Educate the Girl Child) to achieve this record.

4. Largest Envelope - In tribute to the Indian Prime Minister's "Make in India" initiative, Dr. Pillai created a 4000 square meter envelope using waste paper to achieve this record.

5. Attempted - 70000 Candles on a 210 kg Cake - To celebrate the 70th Indian Independence Day, Dr. Pillai attempted to light 70,000 candles on a 210 kg cake, which was recorded in World Records India.

6. Attempted - Documentary on Dhamek Stupa of Sarnath in 17 Languages - Dr. Pillai attempted to create a documentary on the Dhamek Stupa of Sarnath, dubbing it in 17 different languages. The result of this attempt is currently awaiting confirmation from the Guinness World Records.

He is versatile in Gita teaching. The young generation is fond of his Gita teaching and he has changed the life of many young through his continued motivational boost up and teachings.

He has composed and sung Gayatri Mantra in 1008 different tunes.

He has composed and sung Hanuman Chalisa in 108 different tunes.

He has composed and sung hundreds of Sanskrit Bhajans, Patriotic songs, etc.

He has written and directed so many short films and documentaries for awareness campaigns.

He has done voluntary services to UP Police and Kerala Police to spread awareness campaigns on the various issue through videos and photography.

He is on the path of authoring thousands of books on Indian culture, Indian Temples, and the life of extraordinary people.

It is hard to believe that he has produced and directed more than 100 Documentaries on a particular city (Varanasi) which is done by a single person.

He has helped and guided more than 25 boys and girls to achieve world records through various creative and innovative methods.

A multifaceted person who can apply the best of his intellect using the God-given blessings which have been showered upon every human being granting them an immense capacity to learn, experience, and experiment with many things and do wonders in this world of discrimination and disparities.

He is a teacher and a student at the same time who always learns every day and teaches every day. As a master, his weakness was that he never sticks to a particular subject.

Perhaps this weakness gives him the strength to master any area which he came across.

Each of his days dawned with learning a new topic and he spend most of his time experimenting and researching it.

He is also a selfless social activist and a motivational speaker.

His life was full of struggle, ups and downs, and failures. But he never gave up and faced all his trials and tribulations full of confidence. Today he is a successful young man with a lot of enthusiasm and rich life experience.

He is an efficient Tarot Card Reader, Astro-Vastu Consultant and an excellent singer and composer.

He has sung full Ram Charita Manas 138 hours audio by his own composition. He has also sung the whole Bhagavad-Gita in his own composition with a rhythmic background.

He has also sung "Lokah Samastha Sukhino Bhavantu" in 50 different languages.

Currently working on a detailed and scientific study on Veda, Upanishad, Puranas, Bhagavad Gita, etc.

He has composed and sung Hanuman Chalisa in 108 different compositions and Gayatri Mantra in 1008 different compositions.

Awards

Four Times Guinness World Records, Winner of Mahatma Gandhi Vishwa Shanti Puraskar , Mahatma Gandhi Global Peace Ambassador, Kashi Ratna Award, Dr. APJ Abdul Kalam Motivational Person of the Year 2017, Mother Teresa Award, Indira Gandhi Priyadarshini Award, Bharat Vikas Ratna Award, Udyog Ratna Award, Vigyan Prasar Award, Poorvanchal Ratn Samman.

Preface

Welcome to the mystical world of Manikarnika Ghat, one of the holiest cremation grounds in India and a place of great spiritual significance. Located alongside the sacred river Ganges in the city of Varanasi, this ancient site has been a place of spiritual transformation for countless seekers throughout the ages.

In the summer of 2013, I had the opportunity to spend a month and a half at the Manikarnika Ghat, one of the holiest cremation grounds in the city of Varanasi, India. As a researcher, I was drawn to the rich history and spiritual significance of this sacred place, and I was eager to learn more about the rituals and traditions that took place there.

During my time at the ghat, I had the chance to speak with many of the local people who lived and worked there, and I was struck by their stories and their insights. Some of these stories were deeply moving, while others were humorous or thought-provoking. But all of them gave me a greater understanding of the complexity and beauty of the human experience.

As I listened to these stories, I realized that there was a deep well of wisdom and insight to be found at the Manikarnika Ghat. And so, I began to record these stories, with the hope of sharing them with a wider audience.

The result of my efforts is the book that you hold in your hands. In these pages, you will find a collection of stories that I gathered during my time at the ghat, along with my own reflections on their meaning and significance.

I hope that these stories will offer you a glimpse into the world of the Manikarnika Ghat, and that they will inspire you to think more deeply about the mysteries of life and death.

For many, the sight of the funeral pyres burning day and night can be unsettling, but for those who are willing to delve deeper, the ghat holds many secrets and teachings. It is a place where the veil between life and death is thin, and where the true nature of reality can be glimpsed.

This book is a journey into the heart of Manikarnika Ghat, a place where the mysteries of life and death are explored and the path to enlightenment is revealed. Through the stories and teachings of the Aghori, a monastic order of ascetic Shaivite sadhus who reside at the ghat, we will explore the concept of karma and the transformative power of selfless action.

We will also delve into the hidden dimensions of reality and discover the secrets that lie beyond the flames of the funeral pyres. Along the way, we will encounter seekers like ourselves, people who are searching for meaning and fulfillment in a world that can often seem chaotic and confusing.

As you journey with us through the pages of this book, we invite you to open your heart and mind to the teachings of the Aghori and to the transformative power of Manikarnika Ghat. Whether you are seeking enlightenment, healing, or simply a deeper understanding of the world around you, we hope that this book will provide you with the guidance and inspiration you need to find your way.

So come, let us embark on this journey together, and discover the secrets of the funeral ghat. May your journey be one of enlightenment and transformation.

ONE
A Strange Sight

One evening, a group of tourists visiting Manikarnika Ghat witnessed a strange sight. As they watched, a man wearing a black coat and a fedora hat emerged from the shadows and approached one of the cremation pyres. He looked around furtively before reaching into his coat and pulling out a small, intricately carved wooden box.

As the man placed the box on the pyre, the tourists noticed that the flames began to flicker and dance in a strange way. The man then stepped back and watched as the fire consumed the box, a look of intense concentration on his face.

When the flames died down, the man turned and vanished into the night, leaving the tourists wondering what they had just witnessed.

The next day, the tourists decided to investigate and went to the police with their story. The police were skeptical at first, but eventually they agreed to look into the matter.

After a thorough investigation, the police discovered that the man was a notorious thief who had been on the run for years. It turned out that the box contained a valuable ancient artifact that the thief had stolen from a museum.

The thief was eventually caught and brought to justice, thanks to the eyewitness accounts of the tourists who had witnessed the strange events at Manikarnika Ghat.

TWO

The Stolen Ring

The body of a wealthy businessman had just been cremated at Manikarnika Ghat when a group of mourners noticed something strange. As the ashes were being collected, they noticed that one of the gold wedding bands that the businessman had been cremated with was missing.

At first, the mourners assumed that the ring had simply fallen off during the cremation process, but a closer examination revealed that the ring had been deliberately removed. Someone had tampered with the body and stolen the ring.

The mourners immediately notified the police, who launched an investigation. It didn't take long for them to zero in on a suspect: the businessman's disgruntled former business partner, who had been passed over for a promotion and stood to gain a large sum of money if the businessman's will was contested.

The police were able to recover the stolen ring and gather enough evidence to charge the suspect with tampering with a corpse and theft. Thanks to the observant mourners, justice was served and the businessman's final wishes were honored.

THREE

The Woman's Belly

It was a dark and stormy night at Manikarnika Ghat when the body of a young pregnant woman was brought in for cremation. As the funeral pyre was lit, the mourners noticed that the flames seemed to dance and flicker in a strange way.

Suddenly, they heard a loud cracking sound and the woman's belly burst open, revealing a small newborn baby. The baby was momentarily suspended in the air above the flames, as if held up by an invisible force, before falling back into the pyre.

The mourners were shocked and confused, and many of them believed that they had witnessed a miracle. But a few of them were suspicious and decided to investigate further.

After the funeral, they examined the woman's body and discovered that it had been tampered with. Someone had cut open the woman's womb and removed the baby, then sewn the wound back up in an attempt to cover their tracks.

The mourners went to the police with their findings, and a thorough investigation was launched. It didn't take long for the police to uncover a sinister plot involving a group of black market baby traffickers. The suspects were arrested and brought to justice, thanks to the diligence of the mourners who had witnessed the strange events at Manikarnika Ghat.

FOUR
THE TALISMAN

One evening at Manikarnika Ghat, a group of tourists stumbled upon a strange scene. A group of Aghori sadhus were gathered around a funeral pyre, chanting and performing strange rituals. As the tourists watched in fascination, one of the Aghori approached the pyre and reached into the flames, seemingly unharmed by the heat.

The Aghori retrieved a small, intricately carved stone from the pyre and handed it to the leader of the group, who examined it closely before nodding in approval. The Aghori then placed the stone back into the flames and the group resumed their chanting.

The tourists were intrigued by the strange rituals and decided to investigate further. They learned that the stone was a powerful talisman that was said to grant the Aghori spiritual powers. It was believed that the stone had been passed down through the generations, but no one knew where it had come from or how it had come to be in the possession of the Aghori.

The tourists were determined to uncover the secrets of the stone and set out on a journey to learn more. They traveled throughout India, speaking to scholars and seeking out other Aghori sadhus in the hope of learning more about the mysterious talisman.

In the end, they were able to piece together a story that traced the stone back to an ancient civilization that had been lost to time. The mystery of the stone was finally solved, thanks to the curiosity and determination of the tourists who had witnessed the strange events at Manikarnika Ghat.

FIVE

INNER PEACE

One day at Manikarnika Ghat, a group of Aghori sadhus were performing their rituals when a young man approached them, seeking their help. The man was plagued by negative thoughts and feelings, and he believed that the Aghori might be able to help him find inner peace.

The Aghori listened to the man's story and nodded in understanding. They knew that negativity could be a powerful force, but they also believed that it could be overcome with the right mindset.

The Aghori offered the man a special potion that they claimed would help him let go of his negative thoughts and embrace positivity. The man gratefully accepted the potion and drank it down.

To the surprise of the Aghori and the man, the potion had an unexpected side effect: it caused the man to see the world in a completely different way. Suddenly, everything was infused with a sense of wonder and magic. The man saw the beauty in the simplest things and felt a deep connection to the world around him.

The Aghori were puzzled by the strange effect of the potion, and they set out to learn more. They experimented with different ingredients and concoctions, trying to understand what had caused the unexpected transformation in the young man.

In the end, they discovered that the potion had been imbued with the power of positivity, and that it had the ability to change the way people saw the world. The Aghori were thrilled by their discovery and shared their findings with others, hoping to spread the power of positivity to all those in need.

SIX

EVIL AND GOODNESS

One day at Manikarnika Ghat, a group of tourists stumbled upon a strange scene. An Aghori sadhu was sitting by a funeral pyre, his eyes closed in deep concentration. As the tourists watched, the Aghori began to speak in a low, rhythmic voice, as if in a trance.

The Aghori claimed to have the power to see into the hearts of men and discern their true nature. He said that he could sense the presence of goodness and evil in people, and that he could use his powers to guide them towards the light.

The tourists were skeptical at first, but they were also intrigued. They decided to test the Aghori's powers by bringing him a group of volunteers and asking him to determine their true natures.

To the surprise of the tourists and the volunteers, the Aghori was able to accurately discern the inner goodness or evil of each person. He seemed to possess a sixth sense that allowed him to see beyond the surface and into the depths of the human soul.

The tourists were amazed by the Aghori's powers and decided to learn more about his abilities. They spent hours talking to him and learning about his beliefs and practices, and in the end, they left Manikarnika Ghat with a newfound appreciation for the mysteries of the human spirit.

SEVEN

MAN'S WILL

One evening at Manikarnika Ghat, a young man's body was brought in for cremation. The man's family was devastated by his sudden death and gathered at the ghat to pay their respects.

As the funeral pyre was being prepared, a heated argument broke out among the man's relatives. It seemed that there was a disagreement over the man's will, with some family members claiming that it had been altered in their favor while others insisted that it was invalid.

The argument grew more and more intense, with accusations and insults flying back and forth. It was clear that there was a deep rift within the family, and that the man's death had only served to widen it.

The funeral was postponed as the family members tried to resolve their differences, but it seemed that they were unable to come to an agreement. In the end, the man's body was cremated without the presence of his family, who were too divided to come together and say goodbye.

The mystery of the disputed will remained unsolved, and the man's family was left to wonder if their own greed and envy had contributed to his untimely death.

EIGHT

DIVERSITY

One day at Manikarnika Ghat, a group of tourists came across a strange sight. A group of people from all walks of life were gathered around a funeral pyre, watching as the body of a wealthy businessman was cremated.

As the flames consumed the body, the tourists couldn't help but notice the diversity of the mourners. There were rich and poor, young and old, people of all races and religions.

As they watched, the tourists realized that despite their differences, the mourners were all united in their grief. They saw that at the time of death, all of the petty distinctions that separated people - their egos, their status, their prejudices - were meaningless.

The tourists were moved by the realization that in death, all people were equal. They left Manikarnika Ghat with a renewed sense of understanding and a determination to live their lives with compassion and understanding for all people, regardless of their differences.

NINE

NOT CATCHING FIRE.

One day at Manikarnika Ghat, a group of funeral workers were preparing to cremate the body of an elderly man. As they stacked the wood and set the pyre alight, they noticed that the body was not catching fire.

The workers tried everything they could think of to get the fire to spread to the body, but nothing seemed to work. The body remained untouched by the flames, as if protected by some unseen force.

The workers were puzzled and a bit unnerved by the strange occurrence, and they began to wonder if the man was some kind of special being. They consulted with the family and the local priests, but no one had an explanation for the phenomenon.

In the end, the workers decided to bury the body in the ground instead of cremating it. They dug a grave and laid the man to rest, still unsure of what had caused the body to resist the flames.

The mystery of the unburnable body remained unsolved, and the workers were left to wonder if they would ever encounter such a strange occurrence again.

TEN

MISSING SON

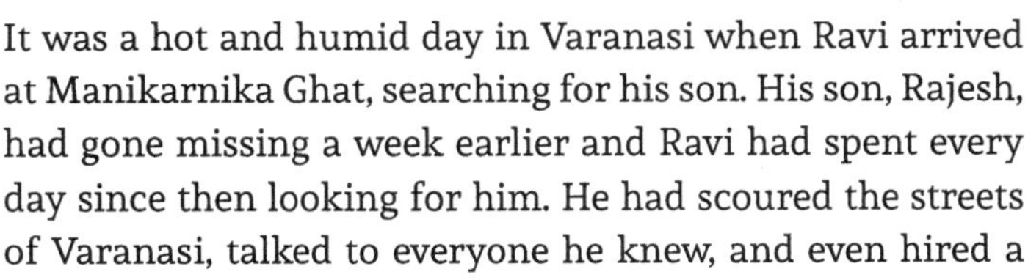

It was a hot and humid day in Varanasi when Ravi arrived at Manikarnika Ghat, searching for his son. His son, Rajesh, had gone missing a week earlier and Ravi had spent every day since then looking for him. He had scoured the streets of Varanasi, talked to everyone he knew, and even hired a private investigator, but he had turned up no leads.

As Ravi walked along the crowded riverfront, his heart heavy with worry, he couldn't shake the feeling that he was getting closer to finding his son. He had always been a deeply spiritual man, and he believed that the gods were guiding him towards his son.

As he approached the cremation grounds, Ravi noticed a group of people gathered around one of the pyres. He pushed his way through the crowd and saw a body lying on the pyre, covered in flowers.

Ravi's heart raced as he approached the body and saw that it was his son, Rajesh. He couldn't believe that his search had led him to this moment, and he fell to his knees, tears streaming down his face.

The mourners gathered around Ravi, trying to console him, but he couldn't hear their words. He was consumed by grief and guilt, blaming himself for his son's death. He had always been a strict father, pushing Rajesh to succeed and often criticizing him for not living up to his expectations. Ravi realized that he had driven his son away with his demanding ways, and now it was too late to make amends.

As the mourners prepared to light the pyre, Ravi stood up and approached the body of his son. He placed his hand on Rajesh's forehead and whispered a prayer, asking for his forgiveness and promising to spend the rest of his days honoring his memory.

As the flames began to rise, Ravi felt a sense of peace wash over him. He knew that his son's spirit was finally at rest, and that he would be reunited with him in the next life.

The mystery of Rajesh's disappearance was solved, but the pain of his loss would stay with Ravi forever. He vowed to use his grief as a reminder to always show love and understanding to those around him, and to never take a single moment for granted.

ELEVEN

PURSUIT OF SUCCESS

One day at Manikarnika Ghat, a lone figure could be seen walking towards the cremation grounds. His name was Rajiv, and he had come to the ghat in search of peace.

Rajiv had always been a driven and ambitious man, but his pursuit of success had come at a great cost. He had fought with his wife over dowry and property, and their marriage had suffered as a result.

As Rajiv walked along the riverfront, he couldn't shake the feeling that he had made a terrible mistake. He had allowed his greed and ego to blind him, and now he was lost and alone.

As he approached the cremation grounds, Rajiv saw a group of mourners gathered around a pyre. He watched as the body of an elderly man was cremated, and he was struck by the sense of finality and closure that seemed to surround the scene.

Rajiv decided that he too wanted to find peace and closure, and he approached the mourners, asking if he could join them in their rituals. The mourners, seeing the pain and remorse on Rajiv's face, welcomed him into their group.

As Rajiv participated in the cremation rites, he felt a sense of peace wash over him. He realized that death was a natural and inevitable part of life, and that it was time to let go of his ego and embrace his mortality.

After the cremation, Rajiv returned home a changed man. He apologized to his wife for his past mistakes and vowed to spend the rest of his days making amends. The mystery of Rajiv's transformation was solved, and he and his wife were able to rebuild their relationship and find true happiness.

TWELVE

MEANINGLESS THINGS

As the sun set over Manikarnika Ghat, a young man named Rohit sat on the riverbank, watching the funeral pyres burn. Rohit had always been curious about death and the afterlife, and he had come to the ghat to learn more about the Hindu cremation rituals.

As Rohit watched the bodies being cremated, he was struck by the sense of peace and acceptance that seemed to radiate from the mourners. He saw that death was a natural and inevitable part of life, and that it was possible to find meaning and purpose even in the face of loss.

Rohit's mind was transformed by what he saw at the ghat, and he began to see the world in a different way. He realized that the material possessions and status that he had always pursued were meaningless in the grand scheme of things, and that true happiness came from within.

As the night wore on, Rohit felt a sense of liberation wash

over him. He had always been weighed down by his fears and insecurities, but now he felt free. He knew that he had found the answers he had been seeking, and he left Manikarnika Ghat with a sense of peace and purpose.

The mystery of Rohit's transformation was solved, and he knew that he would never be the same again. He had discovered a new way of looking at the world, and he was determined to live his life in a way that was true to his newfound beliefs.

THIRTEEN

SAVING A GIRL

As the sun set over Manikarnika Ghat, a young girl named Priya could be seen running through the crowded riverfront, pursued by a man. Priya was terrified, and she didn't know where to turn for help.

The man chasing Priya was a stranger, and she had no idea what he wanted from her. She had been walking home from school when he had suddenly appeared out of nowhere and grabbed her by the arm.

Priya had managed to break free and run, but the man was fast and determined. She had no choice but to keep running, hoping that someone would come to her aid.

As Priya passed the cremation grounds, she saw a group of mourners gathered around a funeral pyre. She hesitated for a moment, unsure if she should seek help from strangers, but then the man grabbed her again and she knew she had no choice.

Priya ran up to the mourners and begged for their help, and

they immediately sprang into action. They chased the man away and brought Priya back to safety, and she collapsed in tears, grateful for their kindness.

As Priya told her story, the mourners listened with shock and outrage. They had seen many things in their time at the ghat, but they had never encountered such a heartless predator. They vowed to do everything in their power to bring the man to justice.

The mystery of Priya's ordeal was solved, and she knew that she would never forget the kindness of the strangers who had helped her. She left Manikarnika Ghat with a renewed sense of hope and faith in the goodness of humanity.

FOURTEEN
A Dog's Funeral

As the sun rose over Manikarnika Ghat, a small group of mourners could be seen gathered around a funeral pyre. They were there to pay their respects to a beloved dog named Rascal, who had lived at the ghat for many years.

Rascal had always been a fixture at the cremation grounds, and everyone who knew him loved him. He was a friendly and affectionate dog, and he brought joy and comfort to all who encountered him.

As the mourners watched the flames consume Rascal's body, they were filled with sadness and grief. They knew that they would never see Rascal again, and they struggled to come to terms with his loss.

Despite their sorrow, the mourners also felt a sense of gratitude and appreciation for Rascal's life. They knew that he had brought joy and love to the ghat, and they were determined to give him a proper funeral in tribute to the special bond they had shared.

As the flames died down and the ashes cooled, the mourners said their final goodbyes to Rascal. They knew that he would always be remembered and loved, and that his spirit would live on in the hearts of all who had known him.

The mystery of Rascal's passing was solved, but the grief of his loss lingered on. The mourners left the ghat with heavy hearts, but also with the knowledge that Rascal had touched their lives in a profound and lasting way.

FIFTEEN
TANTRIK

As the moon rose over Manikarnika Ghat, a person could be seen approaching the cremation grounds. He was a tantrik, a mysterious and powerful figure known for his knowledge of the occult.

The tantrik was a solitary figure, and few people knew why he had come to the ghat. Some said that he was searching for enlightenment, while others whispered that he was seeking to unleash dark and ancient powers.

As the tantrik walked through the ghat, he was watched by the shadows. He seemed indifferent to the stares of the mourners, and he moved with an otherworldly grace.

As he reached the center of the ghat, the tantrik stopped and raised his hands to the sky. He began to chant in a strange and ancient language, and the air around him seemed to shimmer with power.

The mourners watched in awe as the tantrik performed his rituals, and they could feel the energy of the ghat shifting and changing. Some were filled with fear and left the ghat as quickly as they could, but others were drawn to the tantrik and stayed to witness his rituals.

As the tantrik finished his rituals and disappeared into the night, the mourners were left to wonder what had just happened. Some said that they had witnessed a miracle, while others said that they had witnessed a glimpse of the beyond.

The mystery of the tantrik's visit to the ghat remained unsolved, and the mourners left the ghat with many questions on their minds. Some whispered that the tantrik had brought a message from the gods, while others said that he had unleashed a dark and dangerous force.

As the years passed, the tantrik's visit to the ghat became a legend, and many people came to the ghat in search of enlightenment or to seek the tantrik's blessings. Some said that they had seen the tantrik again, performing his rituals at midnight, while others claimed to have received visions or prophecies from him.

To this day, the mystery of the tantrik's visit to Manikarnika Ghat remains unsolved, and his legend continues to inspire and intrigue those who seek the secrets of the beyond.

SIXTEEN
TRUE LOVE

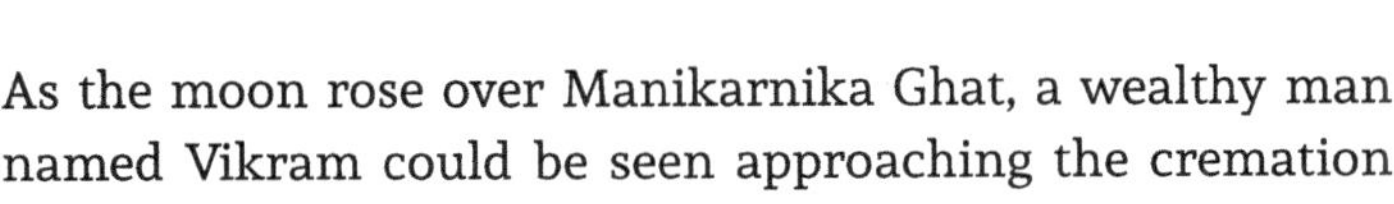

As the moon rose over Manikarnika Ghat, a wealthy man named Vikram could be seen approaching the cremation grounds. He was a well-known figure in the city, and he was known for his lavish parties and opulent lifestyle.

But on this night, Vikram was not seeking pleasure. He was seeking redemption. He had realized that his wealth had brought him nothing but loneliness and emptiness, and he had come to the ghat to make amends.

As Vikram approached the cremation grounds, he was met by a group of mourners. They saw the sadness in his eyes and asked if they could help him. Vikram hesitated for a moment, then opened his suitcase and revealed a mountain of cash.

"I cannot buy love and affection with this money," Vikram said. "The people who loved me only did so because of my wealth. This money has no use if it cannot buy true love."

The mourners were shocked by Vikram's words, and they watched in silence as he handed the suitcase to the cremation worker. "Please burn this as you would a funeral," Vikram said. "I want to rid myself of this curse."

As the flames consumed the money, Vikram felt a weight lifted from his shoulders. He knew that he could not buy back the love and respect he had lost, but he hoped that by renouncing his wealth, he could find peace and redemption.

The mystery of Vikram's transformation was solved, and he left the ghat with a new sense of purpose. He knew that he had a long way to go, but he was determined to make amends for his past mistakes and live a life of honesty and integrity.

SEVENTEEN

MYSTERY OF POWERS

As the sun set over Manikarnika Ghat, a group of mourners gathered around a funeral pyre. They had come to pay their respects to their loved one, and to bid them farewell on their journey to the beyond.

As the mourners watched the flames consume the body, they were startled by the sudden appearance of a tantrik. He was a mysterious and powerful figure, known for his knowledge of the occult and his ability to harness magical powers.

The tantrik approached the mourners and told them that he had a message from the beyond. He said that their loved one was at peace, and that they had a special mission to fulfill in the world of the living.

The mourners were skeptical at first, but as the tantrik spoke, they began to feel a sense of peace and understanding wash over them. They knew that the tantrik was telling the truth, and they were grateful for his words of comfort.

As the tantrik left the ghat, the mourners were left to wonder about the mystery of his powers. Some said that he was a messenger from the gods, while others said that he was a conduit for the spirits of the dead.

To this day, the mystery of the tantrik's powers remains unsolved, and many people continue to seek his guidance and wisdom.

EIGHTEEN

What Happens to the Soul After Death

One day at Manikarnika Ghat, a young student named Rohit approached an Aghori who was sitting by the cremation grounds. The Aghori was a monastic order of ascetic Shaivite sadhus, known for their knowledge of the beyond and their ability to communicate with the spirits of the dead.

Rohit had always been fascinated by the mysteries of life and death, and he had come to the ghat to seek answers from the Aghori. He approached the Aghori and asked him the following questions:

"What happens to the soul after death?"

The Aghori replied, "Death is not the end. It is a passage to another realm, where the soul is free to explore and experience new things."

"Is there a heaven or a hell?"

The Aghori replied, "There are many different realms beyond death, and the soul can choose which path to take. Some believe in the existence of heaven and hell, but it is up to the individual to decide their own destiny."

"Can the dead communicate with the living?"

The Aghori replied, "It is possible for the dead to communicate with the living, through dreams, visions, or other forms of spiritual communication. However, it is important to remember that the dead have their own journey to pursue, and they may not always be able to respond to the requests of the living."

"What is the purpose of life?"

The Aghori replied, "The purpose of life is to learn, grow, and experience all that the world has to offer. It is up to each individual to find their own path and purpose in life."

"Is there a way to cheat death?"

The Aghori replied, "Death is a natural part of the cycle of life, and it is something that we must all eventually face. It is not possible to cheat death, but it is possible to find peace and acceptance in the face of death."

As the Aghori finished speaking, Rohit felt his mind expand with new understanding. He knew that he had much more to learn, but he was grateful for the Aghori's wisdom and guidance.

The mystery of life and death remained unsolved, but Rohit left the ghat with a new sense of purpose and a thirst for knowledge. He knew that he had much more to The Aghori watched as Rohit walked away from the ghat, his mind filled with new insights and questions. He knew that Rohit was just one of many who came seeking answers about the mysteries of life and death, and he was grateful to be able to provide guidance and comfort to those who needed it.

As the Aghori sat by the cremation grounds, he reflected on the many mysteries of the world. He knew that there were many things that remained unexplained, and he was content to let the mysteries unfold in their own time.

For the Aghori, the ghat was a place of peace and contemplation, where the veil between the worlds was thin and the spirits of the dead could be heard. It was a place where the mysteries of life and death could be explored and understood, and where the living could find solace and comfort in the face of loss.

And so, as the sun set over Manikarnika Ghat, the Aghori sat in silence, lost in thought and contemplation, surrounded by the spirits of the dead and the mystery of the beyond.

NINETEEN

A Tourist and a Funeral man

Question and answer session between a tourist and a funeral man at Manikarnika Ghat:

Tourist: "Hello, sir. I see that you have been burning bodies here for the past 40 years. Can you tell me about your experience?"

Funeral man: "Yes, I have been working at this ghat for many years. It has been a privilege to serve the families of the deceased and help them through their time of loss."

Tourist: "What have you learned from your time here?"

Funeral man: "I have learned that death is a natural part of life, and it is something that we must all eventually face. I have also learned that it is important to show respect and reverence for the dead, and to perform the cremation rituals with care and devotion."

Tourist: "Do you believe in the afterlife?"

Funeral man: "I believe that the soul lives on after the body dies. It is a belief that brings comfort to many people, and it is something that I have seen firsthand during my time here at the ghat."

Tourist: "Have you ever experienced any strange or paranormal events during a cremation?"

Funeral man: "There have been times when I have felt the presence of the deceased during a cremation. It is a feeling that is difficult to explain, but it is one that stays with me. I believe that the spirits of the dead are always with us, and that they are watching over us from the beyond."

Tourist: "Thank you for sharing your experiences with me. Your words have been very enlightening."

Funeral man: "You are welcome. I am glad that I could help you understand more about the mysteries of death and the afterlife. May your journey be filled with peace and understanding."

TWENTY
DANCING FLAMES

It was a hot and humid day at the cremation grounds of Manikarnika Ghat, and the funeral pyres were burning brightly under the midday sun. As the funeral workers went about their duties, preparing the bodies for cremation, a strange thing happened.

As they placed the body of an elderly man onto the pyre, they noticed that the flames seemed to be drawn to the body, flickering and dancing around it in a way that was unlike anything they had ever seen before.

The funeral workers watched in amazement as the flames consumed the body, and they began to hear strange noises coming from within the pyre. It sounded like the man was trying to speak, as if he had something important to say.

The funeral workers listened intently, but they could not make out the words. They could only watch as the flames continued to burn, until there was nothing left of the body but a few ashes and bones.

When the funeral workers told the story of what had happened, people were amazed and frightened. Some said that it was a sign from the beyond, a message from the spirit of the deceased. Others said that it was just a trick of the heat and the smoke, and that there was no cause for alarm.

But no matter what anyone said, the funeral workers knew that they had witnessed something truly extraordinary that day at Manikarnika Ghat.

ᑭᑭᑭ

TWENTY-ONE
YOUNG SISTER

As the sun rose over Manikarnika Ghat, a young boy arrived with a shrouded body in his arms. His name was Ravi, and he had traveled all the way from his village to the holiest of cremation grounds, alone and on foot.

Ravi's sister, Pooja, had died suddenly the night before, and he had made the journey to the ghat to fulfill her final wishes. Pooja had always told him that she wanted to be cremated at Manikarnika Ghat, and Ravi was determined to fulfill her wishes, no matter what.

But as Ravi approached the funeral pyres, he was confronted with a problem. He had no money to pay for the cremation, and he knew that he would be turned away if he could not come up with the funds.

Desperate and alone, Ravi approached the funeral workers and begged for their help. "Please, sirs," he said, tears streaming down his face. "I have no money, but my sister's body must be cremated. She was all I had left in the world, and now she is gone. I beg of you, please help me."

The funeral workers were moved by Ravi's plea, and they knew that they had to do something to help. They gathered around Ravi and his sister's body, and they vowed to do whatever it took to make sure that Pooja received a proper cremation.

As word of Ravi's plight spread, more and more people came forward to offer their help. Some gave money, while others donated flowers or rice for the funeral pyre. And as the funeral pyre burned brightly, Ravi felt a sense of peace and comfort wash over him.

In the end, it was a simple act of kindness that made all the difference for Ravi and his sister. And as he watched the flames consume Pooja's body, he knew that she was finally at rest, and that she would always be with him, in his heart.

As the ashes of Pooja's body drifted away on the breeze, Ravi felt a sense of closure and acceptance wash over him. He knew that his sister was finally at peace, and that she was in a better place.

And as he turned to thank the people who had helped him, Ravi saw a face that he recognized. It was Mr. Singh, the wealthy businessman who lived in his village. Mr. Singh had always been kind to Ravi and his sister, and Ravi was grateful to see him at the ghat.

"Thank you, Mr. Singh," Ravi said, as he approached the man. "Thank you for everything."

Mr. Singh smiled and placed a comforting hand on Ravi's

shoulder. "It was the least I could do, my boy," he said. "Your sister was a kind and generous soul, and she deserved a proper funeral. I'm just glad that I could help."

Ravi nodded, tears of gratitude welling up in his eyes. "Thank you," he said again, before turning and walking away from the ghat, his heart a little lighter.

As Ravi made his way back to his village, he knew that he would never forget his journey to Manikarnika Ghat. It was a journey that had brought him face to face with the mysteries of life and death, and it was a journey that had changed him forever. And as he walked on, he knew that he would always carry the memory of his sister and the kindness of the people he had met at the ghat with him, wherever he went.

TWENTY-TWO
GUIDING LIGHT

As the funeral pyre burned at Manikarnika Ghat, a young man stood by, tears streaming down his face. His name was Rohit, and he had just lost his father, the man who had been his rock and his guiding light.

Rohit's father had always been a responsible and caring man, and Rohit had learned so much from him over the years. He had been the one who held the family together, and Rohit knew that he would never be able to fill the void left by his father's absence.

As the days passed, Rohit found himself unable to leave the ghat. He stayed by the pyre, day and night, lost in memories of his father and all that he had meant to him. He remembered the lessons his father had taught him, the wisdom he had imparted, and the love he had always shown him.

As the week wore on, Rohit's family began to worry about him. They came to the ghat, urging him to come home and rest. But Rohit couldn't bring himself to leave. He felt a deep connection to his father at the ghat, and he couldn't bring himself to let go.

It was the people at the ghat who finally helped Rohit find the strength to move on. They saw the pain and the grief in his eyes, and they knew that he needed to find a way to heal. They offered him words of comfort and advice, and they helped him see that his father would want him to carry on and live his life to the fullest.

With their help, Rohit finally found the courage to let go and move on. He said goodbye to his father and to the ghat, and he returned home to his family, his heart a little lighter.

As he looked back on his time at the ghat, Rohit knew that he would always carry the memories of his father and the kindness of the people he had met there with him, wherever he went. And as he looked to the future, he knew that he would always be grateful for the love and the guidance his father had given him, and for the strength he had found at Manikarnika Ghat.

TWENTY-THREE

AGHORI'S OCCULT POWER

One day in the evening at Manikarnika Ghat, a lone figure emerged from the shadows. It was an "Aghori," a monastic order of ascetic Shaivite sadhus known for their extreme rituals and their powerful occult powers.

The Aghori approached the funeral pyres, his eyes glowing with an otherworldly light. He was searching for something, something that only he knew about. And as he moved closer to the pyres, he knew that he was getting closer to what he sought.

As he reached the pyres, the Aghori stopped and closed his eyes. He raised his hands to the sky, and he began to chant an ancient incantation. The words flowed from his lips like a river of fire, and as he spoke them, the pyres began to burn brighter and brighter.

The Aghori's chanting grew louder and more intense, and the flames of the pyres rose higher and higher. And then, suddenly, the Aghori stopped. He opened his eyes, and he looked straight at the flames.

In that moment, something emerged from the pyres. It was a shadowy figure, a being of pure darkness and malevolence. It stared at the Aghori with eyes of fire, and it let out a blood-curdling scream.

The Aghori did not flinch. He stood his ground, his eyes fixed on the shadowy figure. And then, with a flick of his wrist, he sent a bolt of energy hurtling towards the being.

The bolt hit its mark, and the shadowy figure let out a final, tortured cry. It collapsed to the ground, and as it did, it vanished in a puff of smoke.

The Aghori let out a sigh of relief, and he turned to leave. As he walked away from the pyres, he knew that he had faced one of the most powerful and malevolent beings in the world, and he had emerged victorious.

But as he made his way back to his cave, the Aghori couldn't shake the feeling that this was not the last he would see of the shadowy figure. He knew that it would be back, and he knew that he would have to be ready when it returned.

TWENTY-FOUR

SEEING PAST LIFE

As the sun began to set over Manikarnika Ghat, a young man approached an "Aghori" who was sitting by the funeral pyres. The Aghori was a monastic order of ascetic Shaivite sadhus known for their extreme rituals and their powerful occult powers.

The young man, whose name was Rohan, had heard about the Aghori's powers and had come to seek his advice. Rohan was at a crossroads in his life, and he wasn't sure which path to take. He had always dreamed of a successful career and a comfortable life, but he wasn't sure if that was the right path for him.

As Rohan approached the Aghori, he bowed his head in respect. The Aghori looked up at him, his eyes glowing with an otherworldly light. Without a word, he held out his hand to Rohan.

Rohan hesitated for a moment, but then he placed his hand in the Aghori's. The Aghori closed his eyes, and as he did, Rohan felt a surge of energy flow through his body. It was as if the Aghori was looking deep into his soul, seeing all of his past lives and all of his karmas.

When the Aghori opened his eyes, he looked at Rohan with a mixture of compassion and concern. "Your karmas from your past lives are weighing heavily on you," he said. "You have done much harm in your previous incarnations, and you must work to reconcile that harm in this lifetime.

Rohan was shocked by the Aghori's words. He had never thought about his past lives or the impact they might have on his present. But as the Aghori spoke, he knew that the old man was right.

"What can I do?" Rohan asked, his voice trembling.

The Aghori smiled gently. "You must do good karma," he said. " "You must help others and act with compassion and kindness. Only then will you be able to balance the scales and find peace in this life. It will not be easy, but if you are dedicated and sincere, you can achieve it."

Rohan nodded, understanding the weight of the Aghori's words. He knew that he had a long journey ahead of him, but he was ready to face it. He thanked the Aghori for his guidance and turned to leave.

As he walked away from the pyres, Rohan knew that he had been given a second chance. He vowed to use it wisely and to live his life in a way that would honor his past and bring peace to his future. And with that, he set off on a new path, determined to make the most of his time on earth.

TWENTY-FIVE

PATH TO ENLIGHTENMENT

As the sun rose over Manikarnika Ghat, a group of tourists approached an "Aghori" who was sitting by the funeral pyres. The Aghori was a monastic order of ascetic Shaivite sadhus known for their extreme rituals and their powerful occult powers.

The tourists, who were all seeking spiritual enlightenment, asked the Aghori if he could share some wisdom with them. The Aghori looked at them with kind eyes and nodded.

"The path to enlightenment begins with understanding the concept of karma," the Aghori said. "Karma is the result of our actions, and it determines the circumstances of our present and future lives. There are two types of karma: selfish action, or "karmas," and selfless action, or "karmas."

"Selfish actions are driven by ego and desire, and they create negative karma. They bring suffering and difficulties in our lives. On the other hand, selfless actions are those that are done with the intention of helping others, and they create positive karma. They bring happiness and fulfillment."

The tourists listened intently, soaking up the Aghori's words. They knew that they had much to learn, and they were grateful for the opportunity to learn from such a wise and enlightened being.

"So the key to happiness and enlightenment is to focus on selfless action," the Aghori continued. "By doing good deeds and helping others, we create positive karma that will bring joy and fulfillment to our lives. Remember, the path to enlightenment is not an easy one, but it is worth the journey."

The tourists thanked the Aghori for his teachings and promised to remember his words as they continued on their spiritual journey. And with that, they left the ghat, filled with hope and determination to live their lives in a way that would bring them closer to enlightenment. As the tourists walked away from the Aghori, they were filled with a sense of purpose and direction. They knew that they had much to learn, but they were ready to embrace the challenge.

Over the next few days, they explored the city of Varanasi and learned about the various spiritual practices and rituals that were followed by the people there. They visited temples, participated in prayer sessions, and meditated by the Ganges River.

But most importantly, they focused on selfless action. They helped those in need, offering food and assistance to the poor and the sick. They gave generously to charities and worked to make a difference in the world.

As they practiced selfless action, the tourists began to feel a sense of inner peace and contentment. They knew that they were on the right path, and they were grateful for the guidance of the Aghori and the lessons they had learned at Manikarnika Ghat.

And as they continued on their journey, they knew that they were one step closer to enlightenment, and that they were making the world a better place in the process.

TWENTY-SIX

True Spiritual Master.

As the sun began to set over the holy city of Varanasi, a small crowd of people began to gather at the banks of the Ganges River. They had heard rumors of an Aghori, a monastic order of ascetic Shaivite sadhus, who was known for his deep understanding of the spiritual teachings of the Kathopanishad.

The Aghori arrived at the ghat, his body covered in ash and his mind focused on the divine. He took his place on a raised platform and began to speak, his words carrying across the water to the ears of the gathered crowd.

"The Kathopanishad teaches us that the ultimate goal of life is to merge with the divine and to become one with the absolute," he said. "But how do we attain this state of unity? The answer lies in the understanding of the true nature of the self."

As the Aghori spoke, the crowd listened intently, hanging on every word. They had never heard such wisdom before, and they knew that they were in the presence of a true spiritual master.

The Aghori continued, explaining the concept of "atman" and the journey of the soul towards ultimate realization. He spoke of the importance of detachment and the power of selfless action, and he encouraged the people to seek their own inner wisdom and to follow their own path towards enlightenment.

As the evening drew to a close, the Aghori concluded his teaching and the crowd dispersed, each person feeling a sense of peace and understanding. They knew that they had been touched by something special, and they left the ghat with a renewed sense of purpose and dir**ection.**

TWENTY-SEVEN

CHARISMA OF AN AGHORI

The Aghori was a strange and mysterious figure, known for his unconventional ways and his deep understanding of the spiritual teachings of the ancient scriptures. He was often seen wandering the streets of Varanasi, particularly around the sacred cremation ground of Manikarnika Ghat.

Despite his strange appearance, with his body covered in ash and his hair matted and wild, the Aghori had a certain charisma that drew people to him. They were drawn by his words of wisdom and his insights into the mysteries of life and death.

As he roamed the streets, the Aghori would often stop and speak to those he encountered, sharing his wisdom and teachings with anyone who would listen. He had a particular talent for singing, and he would often break into song as he walked, his voice carrying across the crowded streets.

"People are fools," he would sing. "They don't know what they are gathering, and for what. Ultimately, they have to come here and go empty-handed."

Some people found the Aghori's words disturbing, but others were fascinated by his insights. They would gather around him, hanging on his every word as he shared his teachings.

In these moments, the Aghori would speak of the importance of ethical living and the power of selfless action. He would tell stories of those who had lived exemplary lives, and he would encourage his listeners to follow their own path towards enlightenment.

Despite his unconventional appearance and his unconventional ways, there was no denying the wisdom and insight of the Aghori. His words touched the hearts of all who heard them, and they left his presence feeling uplifted and inspired.

As the years passed, the Aghori's reputation grew, and people came from far and wide to hear his teachings. He became a fixture of the streets of Varanasi, a beacon of light and wisdom in a world that can often seem dark and confusing.

And though he was but a humble monk, the Aghori's teachings echoed through the ages, inspiring countless people to seek their own path towards enlightenment and to live a life of purpose and meaning.

For the Aghori, the journey towards enlightenment was a

never-ending one, and he was always seeking new ways to deepen his understanding of the mysteries of life and death. He spent long hours in meditation, seeking to connect with the divine and to understand the true nature of reality.

And even as he grew older and his physical body began to show the signs of age, the Aghori remained as vibrant and as full of life as ever. His mind was sharp and his spirit was strong, and he continued to roam the streets of Varanasi, sharing his wisdom and teachings with anyone who would listen.

Despite the challenges that he faced, the Aghori remained true to his path and to his purpose. And in the end, it was this unwavering dedication that earned him the respect and admiration of all who knew him.

For the Aghori, there was no greater joy than to share his wisdom and to help others find their own path towards enlightenment. And as he walked the streets of Varanasi, singing his songs of wisdom and offering his insights to all who would listen, he knew that he was fulfilling his destiny and living a life of true purpose and meaning.

Other Books Of The Author

1. The Moments When I Met God
2. Kashiyile Theertha Pathangal
3. GURU GYAN VANI
4. Abhiprerak Gita
5. ASSI SE JAIN GHAT TAK
6. Hopelessness of Arjuna
7. The Soul and It's True Nature
8. Sense of Action (Karma)
9. Action through Wisdom
10. Action through Wisdom
11. THEORY AND PRACTICAL OF EVERY ACTION
12. LOGICAL UNDERSTANDING OF THE SUPREME
13. THE IMPERISHABLE SUPREME
14. Yatra Nishadraj se Hanuman Ghat Tak
15. Yatra Karnatak Ghat se Raja Ghat Tak
16. Yatra Pandey Ghat se Prayagraj Ghat Tak
17. Yatra Ranjendra Prasad Ghat se Dattatreya Ghat Tak
18. YaatraSindhiya Ghat se Gwaliar Ghat Tak
19. Yatra Mangala Gauri Ghat se Hanuman Gadhi Ghat Tak
20. Yatra Gaay Ghat Se Nishad Ghat Tak
21. MAA GANGA, GHATEN EVM UTSAV
22. Ganga Arti Dev Deepavali evam Any Utsav
23. Potentials of Digitalized India
24. VEDIC CONSCIOUSNESS
25. A Brief Introduction to Vedic Science
26. Kashi ke Barah Jyotirling
27. IMPACT OF MOTIVATION
28. Let's have a Milky Way Journey
29. Color Therapy in a Nutshell

30. Rigveda in a Nutshell
31. Yajurveda in a Nutshell
32. Samveda in a Nutshell
33. Atharva Veda in a Nutshell
34. Ayushman Bhava - Ayurveda
35. Srimad Bhagavad Gita and Upanishad Connection
36. Srimad Bhagavad Gita - an attempt to summarize each chapter.
37. Facts and Impact of Nakshatra
38. Astro Gems - NAVARATNA
39. Ekadashi - A Concise Overview
40. A Concise View of Hanuman Chalisa
41. Inspirational Gita
42. Nakshatraranyam
43. Summary of 18 Mahapuranas
44. Synopsis of 18 Upa Puranas
45. Rigvediya Upanishads
46. Shukla Yajurvediya Upanishads
47. Krishna Yajurvediya Upanishads
48. Samavediya Upanishads
49. Atharvavediya Upanishads
50. The Seven Great Sages
51. From Rocket Scientist to President Dr. APJ Abdul Kalam
52. The Visionary's Voice - Quotes of Dr. APJ Abdul Kalam
53. The Wisdom of Swami Vivekananda: Insights and Inspiration from a Legendary Spiritual Teacher
54. Ayurvedic Remedies from the Garden
55. Sages and Seers
56. Rising Strong – Motivational Stories of Women

Contact

DR. JAGADEESH PILLAI

PhD in Vedic Science

Four Times Guinness World Record Holder

Winner of Mahatma Gandhi Vishwa Shanti Puraskar and Global Peace Ambassador

Gemology, Astro & Vastu Consultant - Spiritual Counselor

Consultant for designing World Record Ideas

Efficient Tarot Card Reader

9839093003

myrichindia@gmail.com

drjagadeeshpillai@facebook

drjagadeeshpillai@instagram

jagadeeshpillai@youtube

www. JAGADEESHPILLAI.com

|| LOKAHA SAMSTHAHA SUKHINO BHAVANTU ||

Printed by Libri Plureos GmbH in Hamburg,
Germany